Writing the Stars

writing
the
stars

poems

lou ella hickman

Press 53
Winston-Salem

Press 53, LLC
PO Box 30314
Winston-Salem, NC 27130

First Edition

A Tom Lombardo Poetry Selection

Cover design by Kevin Morgan Watson

Cover art, "Evening Twilight," Copyright © 2024
by Sister Marilyn Springs, OVISS
Used by permision of the artist.

Library of Congress Control Number
2024945331

ISBN 978-1-950413-87-4

to charlene and henry

*in honor of the 400th anniversary
of the foundation of the
Order of the Sisters
of the Incarnate Word
and
Blessed Sacrament*

acknowledgments

The author thanks the ediors of the publications where these poems first appeared.

Al-Khemia Poetica: A Women's Arts and Writing Journal, "a journey"

Arkansas Review, "South Texas farmer's cotton bales slashed by vandals"

Autumn Sky, "the truth of it"

AWP Part II, "for fukushima: during the fifth year of memory"

Blue Collar Review, "bernard marks defend immigrants in sacramento"

Byline Magazine, "Encounter with Anne Sexton's Poems," "for betty with cancer, who asked for a poem," "Kentucky Mystery"

Christian Century, "consummation"

Cloud Women's Quarterly Journal, "mesquite," "spring, a fairy tale"

Commonweal Magaznie, "widow of zarepthath"

Dance Connection, "pale wings"

Disability Rag and Resources, "on your blindness"

Emmanuel, "all saints church of the kitchen table"

National Catholic Reporter, "Election Year"

New Verse News, "Kroger," "the prisoners," "the unspeakable," "vigil"

Pilgrim: A Journal of Catholic Experience, "the flight into egypt"

Plum Tree Tavern, "japanese inn"

Prism: An Interdisciplinary Journal of Holocaust Educators, "encounter with a Shoah survivor corpus christi, texas"

Studio: A Journal of Christian Writing, "writing is such a jealous lover," "if I were given ten lines"

Texas Assignments, "the retired lady in the texas assisted-living facility," "writing the stars"

The Arts in Religion and Theological Studies, "mitzvah: organ donation"

The Drabble, "wild woman waiting: a poet reflects on her craft," "poetry helps, she said"

The Ekphrastic Review, "judith slays holofernes"

The Lucid Stone, "grandfather sky"

The Southern Review, "when the sisters of mercy were nurses during the civil war"

The Stauros Notebook, "poem"

Thimble, "eve after eden," "the trees"

Valley Voices, "texas snow," "The Displaced"

Vineyards, "come rain"

contents

introduction

While I am not an astronaut and have never traveled in space, I can imagine the immense silence one would encounter while floating among the stars—a quietude even more vast and all-encompassing than our earthly experience of silence—something that most human beings tend to avoid. We play our music and our video games, talk on the phone, watch TV, and generally do our best to fill any "gaps" in one-on-one conversation. Not so, however, for Sister Lou Ella Hickman, author of the poetry collection, *Writing the Stars.*

Unlike most of us, rather than avoiding the "discomfort" of stillness and hush, she embraced them and in so doing, was able to gift the world with these fine poems. This is a poet who listens so intently, she can hear what the stars are saying. They speak of intimate moments like sitting with a friend who is dying ("The Final Say"), how one waits patiently for the earth to make green again what fire has consumed and destroyed ("After the Paradise Fire"), and how spring is a promise always kept ("The Trees").

And deep within each of Sister Lou Ella's poems, is a well of mercy such that the chilling effect of star-like, impartial observation, is warmed and humanized by this empathetic poet's touch. In "Texas Snow," the narrator asks, "What do I know of cotton/fields," and "what do I know/ and/what I cannot know/of dark breathings' sweat and tears," which feels like a crying out from an author who can only offer her compassion to those whose brutal labors are done. And in "On Your Blindness," addressed to a premature child, she writes "with fire and water/ you danced a dance/with stars you never saw," again, mixing observation with human feeling.

So, *Writing the Stars* is not simply star-speak, but the culmination of years of empathetic listening to the world weep with joy and with sorrow. Unlike God, we cannot make the Word flesh, but we can mirror His love in our own small ways, whether it be with poetry or song, or by being a loving presence in a time of need. Sister Lou Ella Hickman has drawn upon, time and time again, in her life and in her poetry, the light that shines on and within us all, as well as the soul's longing for connection with others and with our Creator. These poems are not just starlight, but mercy-light—not the Word made flesh, but words made with love.

Terri Kirby Erickson
September 22, 2022

the truth of it

would you believe
the earth round tilted mother
of all living once was jealous
of our desire to fly
perhaps she invented gravity
to hold such attempts to soar
to her flesh we
pinned like butterflies for centuries
she is not indifferent nor blind
with her pull between ocean and moon
she waits   still
with her invisible web

the final say

*The making of a garden requires the same
kind of ruthlessness as the making of a poem.*
—stanley kunitz

it was sometime after dark
when my friend's doctor came in
the patient has the final say
clearly, she did
then the hours into that night brambled their ruthless
silence
clinging to bed sheets
beneath her dying
then the simple moments
when we talked . . . how we would like to die
 then the doctor turned to leave

> *sunny day face down*
> *in my garden embracing the earth*
> she said

such is poem making
ruthless and certain as death

mitzvah: organ donation

now it is called "recover"
when i first read it
i thought
recover?
from what? a cold?
the flu?
then
recover stolen jewelry?
no disrespect intended
but recover?
before that
the word "harvest"
i relished the idea
as a donor
i imagined
my body
a field of golden wheat
simmering with wind and sun
my friend said in hebrew
pikusch nehesh
"to save a life"
the world entire
with a heart lung layer of skin eyes
so someone might breathe touch
see through mine
recover then must do for now
for now my body remains a field
its own world
until the day a farmer and his combine

will harvest wheat
in a cold, white room
quickening with life
then to nourish
another life a world entire

all saints church of the kitchen table

during this forever moment
we give thanks
over coffee, cream and sugar
all things cereal, orange juice
litany of scrambled eggs, bacon, toast bless us
for the altar is spread with mercy each morning
words fleshed sacred to the touch
speaking in tongues of laughter filling saucer and cup
midnight snacks
chanting while opening jars of grandma's pickled okra
across memories, stories that will help bury her
tomorrow children fed growing like wildflowers
around this our meadow with the festival hum of bees
placemats and paper plates fit for the feast
mac and cheese fish sticks and tea paper towels wipe
faces linen clean
sunday and thanksgiving christmas and easter rising
chocolate cake birthdays and ice cream
come dressed in vestments most sacred most holy
pjs, slippers, jeans
come as you are
all are invited to this table
where we are all the citizens
and somewhat saints who psalm imperfectly *amen*
around this our meadow with the festival hum of bees

eight questions for eve after eden

what did you feel when adam first made love to you
did you taste that painful word—desire—
were you frightened as your belly grew round as fruit
when labor induced your screams
did your blood spill on the ground giving birth to cain
then, as you fed your son your body's milk
did you delight in the life you held in your hands . . .
years later how did you learn of abel's murder
the death of your second child
desire born again of adam's heaving
did cain show you the scar of God's fateful promise
finally, what did you feel when you watched him go
a marked and haunted man

among the ashes: a tiny red suitcase found
    after a house fire

in what was left of her room
a tiny suitcase was found
a gift for a child and her doll . . .
the news reported
a dryer short circuited
most people die breathing the smoke
rather than burns
deep among the ashes
a tiny red suitcase
a doll
her body

writing the stars

to addie

night   no moon

during an unknown season
why was i in our family's pasture
no clue
but i *was* there
such is the veil of memory   above me
an infinity of black silk and stars
the beginning
a child's first poem
an unfolding of hunger for black silken stars

for betty, with cancer, who asked for a poem

like you, living
i put pen to paper
not knowing
where the lines will end
i, too, do not know where i am going
until i get there
but the poem is everything
road, map, compass
the very engine driving

Shoah survivor defends immigrants in sacramento march 29, 2017

history, he said, *will not be on your side*

poor little man came the reply
knows nothing of the legalities

yet
when bernard was a child
it was the law who picked him up
sent his family into ashes and smoke swirling up
from ovens created to bake loaves of bread
such was the charred history of hitler's final recipe

the reply continued
it is apples and oranges, really
comparing the Shoah to illegals

few ask why they come
fewer still ask who will pick apples and oranges for $50 a ton

mesquite

distilled hard liquor whose knots coil
and ever slowly
the spun gold sap seeps slow tears under a spear thorn

spring: a fairy tale

once upon a time
the time it was last year
and each year before that
the sky
fell
as predicted
its luscious blue caught
in branches
where
blooming white clouds had gathered
however this year . . .
the almost blue sky falls again
in brittle white ashes

a simple hope for us, the lost

we are the fires roaring out
of our drought of tenderness

we are a bitter cold
a greed that freezes lives

we are the slow choke of plastic that strangles
everything

we do not weep over what we have vanished
so the stars watch us in their cosmic sadness

we are the price for a tomorrow
    we must sit in the silence
    we must sit long enough with a thorned heart
until the universe can find us and bring us home

after the paradise fire:
   november 8 – november 25, 2018

such was the wasteland . . .
the sky was torched
into an orange and yellow wound
left from a season of fire . . .
in this burnt desert
a mirage of water
marked the horizon of evening
and each evening
beckoned a feathered speck
a solitary shadow
gliding over a blackened earth
a dying remnant . . .
will wildness return
to breathe the whispered gift of green

come rain

i will dance in a circle
for drought is a circle of fire ants
and dance in a circle with open arms

come rain
for dust is the feet now of my beloved
and dance in a circle with sad eyes

come rain
i will dance

and roar

come rain

until there is only a whisper

come

rain

the trees

it is autumn
the trees are old and tired here
like a couple whose bed of fifty years
is filled with stories
the trees also whisper their memories
into the fragrance of night . . .
today snow slowly falls at the window
soon spring will breathe again
the couple will continue their stories
as darkness deepens

consummation

earth will have her own way with hunger
green springing up devouring light
roots singing down into darkness seeking water
rivers hurling themselves to the sea
that, too, is hunger
tides eating up shores
falling and rising teased by the moon
and the mountains
mute in their mystery
repaying the eagle and the forest
everything hungers here
even the sand mingling with wind
scours then savors all into nothingness
remember
it is not their plenty or scarcity
that we honor
but desire

pale wings

the other night as i fell asleep
pale wings fluttered in my chest
attracted to some invisible heat and light
night moth
i never noticed you until then
but now
there is more ballet than i dreamed
with every breath
a dance
around around an inner flame

encounter with anne sexton

the hit and run became blind pain
crouching in the corner
of an upholstery shop
i didn't see it
only the brittle space remains
as i manage to get the dog from the street
while the neighborhood children stand speechless
i press down on the dog with a pillow
waiting
i watch through the glass of the door
two ladies go on with their sewing
not even the pillow hides the claws digging into the corner's wood
until they pull from flesh
waiting, i hold him down
until a man took off his belt and made a loop
i still remember holding a pillow
watching him walk away
with a dog hanging from a belt like a noose to
a silent blue truck

now there is you

like a dog in a noose blind in your pain   hanging

"South Texas farmers cotton bales slashed by vandals" August 21, 2019

Corpus Christi Caller

like a knife to gigantic throats
the fifteen rolls of cotton were slit . . .
the night
like dark blood poured over the bare fields
what stars there were
watched in their silence
unlike the many onlookers who heard
the voiceless in their screaming

texas snow

i

what do i know of cotton fields
so many miles of blooming white lines
here in texas we nicknamed it *snow*

ii

from my car window
on a paved highway how many acres
how many fields
do i pass driving in my air-cooled comfort

iii

distance   distant
time called past
when black hands/brown arms pulled these white
blooms
dragged cotton sacks
under a texas july sun
my silence is such a painful distance
what do i know
and
what i cannot know
of dark breathings' sweat and tears

when the sisters of mercy were nurses
     during the civil war

wearing black serge they brought salvation to stench and blood
as they sponged their prayers
over sweating skin, poxed or gutted faces
that were neither blue nor gray
then
they went to feed the blinded their food
a spoonful after spoonful . . .
they windowed grace and solace
after a carpenter's saw severed gangrene's theft of life
some even duty's final blessing of burying the dead
from a diseased or shell-shot crucifixion
then
after four grotesque years
of what seemed to be an eternity of exhaustion ended
they returned to pittsburgh, new york, baltimore
to their convents' voice of bells
and into the silence of our history

the flight into egypt

donkey brown as dust
click clicked across the stones
it must have been spring when they left
she olive dark and child
and he with tallit over fervent shoulders
the wind rustling their robes like leaves
hers pale green and child
both she and child would be hard pressed
in an unknown future
becoming oil to cross foreheads with glistening fire

if i were given only ten lines

and then be forever mute
what story would i unfold
and enfold with words so bright
they sizzled
about lives so lived they are life
how would i show my greatest respect
for each sound, taste, touch each syllable
every pause
to announce this   and this alone
is living

wild woman, waiting

sensuous and melancholy as the wind through moors . . .
she is the poem the jealous lover
we meet at twilight . . .
for our night i am ravished into words
then as i leave her wild, aching embrace
the sun rises gently over fertile, misty fields

on your blindness

to a premature child

when
in a room of whiteness they fed you with
air
they did not know
they burnt your eyes into darkness
then
with fire and water
you danced a dance
with stars you never saw
but heard them falling into your night

eclipse

annulus ring of light
thin as my grandmother's wedding band
i wear now as a religious
how like the dark center
my life
surrounded with light i cannot see
but i know is there

the prisoners

they are prisoners of wars they did not fight
in escaping street and backyard battle
they slip under the unwelcome sign hoping . . .
and for the nameless
the sun dries their bones
who will mourn their slow death
who will mourn their shackled hope

vigil

your child's body stretches out on your lap a pietà

as you remove the thorned crown of thoughts and prayers
        blood slowly crawls down the leg of your chair
then drop by drop marks your vigil on the floor

visitors pass   your silence answers their questions
 the outside darkness fills the window pane
the senator's secretary says

i have to lock up now

you reply

i'll be back tomorrow

a journey

i survived a childhood haunting
until
the unexpected gutted everything glacier
and life collapsed down to a pebble . . .
then, a stone's throw into the future
another ancient gracefulness
appeared an omen in a dream
a spirit animal talisman
carved to fit in the palm of my hand . . .
and now with this poem
i grow into seventy years
survival is a wildness wonder
marked with prowling paw prints
and fresh scat
tonight
a soul-faced she-wolf
flashes across the forest darkness
i hold in my eyes
as i sit in this silence
waiting for the first snow to fall

the retired lady at the texas assisted-living facility

far too simple to say thank you
like a scrap of paper on the floor
or a sidewalk flower
pick up what was dropped
blow the dandelion into wishes
a thousand times thank you
she told me
then she walked away pushing her cane
and her coke bottle bottom glasses gliding
her down the hall
she the small scrap of paper
she the dandelion blown into wishes

election year

today
there is voting in our neighborhood
the cars pull up, ease into the drive and park
the sky is overcast
these are the ordinary the silent the old drab
as the rain that comes and goes
almost as invisible
they enter the school building
each in turn will pull a lever
as if lighting a small votive candle
better than to curse the darkness . . .
too tired for any other kind of prayer
they leave to live beyond any elected promises
but their own
a clunker starts and gurgles down the drive
an epic of some forgotten time
that's the word for it epic
epics endure—
beyond promises no matter how brittle
as a wise man once said
more than survival, somehow, we will endure

the displaced

we, too, are homeless . . .
while some
walk the streets
close to city hall
others sleep in its shadow
at times
during summer
to escape the heat
this early morning sunday quiet
first to arrive
a withered man with a small black and white dog
with a frayed rope for a leash
then
a woman with few teeth and electric shock hair
her nickname *snowflake* . . .
next a man dressed in green plastic
on high alert to voices
as his hands tremble from a distant war
a few others with backpacks and hoodies
one with a scruffy beard pulls out a small
book
he asked for a bible
once
they line up
always *thank you* for the coffee and rolls . . .
unlike the gratitude that blows away like
newsprint
that covered our faces
asleep on a park bench in winter

the year of the strange moons

omens perhaps . . .
the moon casts her nets as she has always done
pulling oceans
pulling our bodies' hidden seas
dredging up our deepest fears

judith slays holofernes

by the beauty of her countenance
disabled him
judith 16:16-18

bible scholars pronounced my story fiction
fiction or not
i am more than a story's heroine
i am lady wisdom herself
proclaiming in my stride
this is how to act, to live
as i walk out the city gate . . .
i am armored with only perfume, silks and lies
when the soldiers let me enter the dreadful camp . . .
biding my time
i stalk my prey
and wait like a circling hawk will wait
knowing full well
my wisdom can only seduce but with beauty
and then
with my beauty
kill

writing is such a jealous lover

demanding in my solitude
in each ravishment absolute attention
then demands yet more
so much more of my passion that each embrace

like a hair shirt

burns

my skin, bones, blood

until they

     drop away leaving bare

     a throbbing

the unspeakable

in memory of sr. dianna ortiz, osu
rape and torture victim

I'm not sure what it means to forgive . . .
the death certificate read cancer
but i know better
the unspeakable terror
that tortured your flesh years ago
has finally had its way with you
then and then daily the Holy in your body
screamed *why have you forsaken me*
when you wrestled the command to forgive

but the Holy will also have Its way

giving voice to the thousands of missing and
	murdered indigenous women both in the
	united states and Canada

for uli

perhaps
if there had been fewer faces
with one or two images that the public could not unsee
with names that would lead to protests
those costly catalysts for change
but there were too many of us for rage . . .
we were sacred life bearers like our mother the earth
and with our deaths
we will also no longer nurture or create beauty
we will never be the beautiful old ones the wisdom guides
as well as the two-spirit women among us
likewise life giving and creative vanish
shot strangled beaten raped
then
left to die
alone
this was our fear
this is now our grief
there are too many of us for rage

japanese inn

wind
blowing seaward

the door opens
i stand
watching the wind

tomorrow
my son will die
the door closes
my bath is ready

for fukushima daiichi:
    during the tenth year of memory

the shore a worthy opponent

faces lost as they inhaled the water the fired-edged sword
faces countless as sand

and the salt plume crashing

faces such faces swirling

haunting

with its stench breathing out of bodies and faces
yet this too a rice field
we will plant with the green stalks of memory

encounter with a Shoah survivor

corpus christi, texas

she stood in front of me
in line at the post office
she was petite, perhaps 4'8" or 9"
yet spry for her age
looking down from my 5'7" height
i could see her hair
so thin on top
i thought she was a cancer survivor
then i noticed her left arm
on the glass counter to the left of us
numbers inked into her skin
since then
when i remember her
i also remember soup lines
ashes and swirling smoke

fairy tale

the moon's silence is the singing no one hears
in the story of the lonely roma
swirling around a fire called earth

---

widow of zarephath

i was like a small bird pecking near a gate
when i went in search of twigs
a bit of wood for a fire
so after one last meal
my son and i could die . . .
        then a man asked for water
                a bit of bread
                now i, a small bird,
                found more than twigs
                because i, like ravens, fed him

unci maka

i want to touch the poems
that come as breath to her
i want to inhale
the smell of her deep green jungle wild and ageless
the first snow's fragrance
perfuming mountain forests
i want to taste
her glistening sugar of stars
scattered on each velvet night
the salt flavor of ocean spray
the grit of desert sand
then
      i want
      to see thru the eye of the sun
          all that she is birthing

unci skan

the flesh of this evening is the cool turquoise sky
singing was the old voice
chanting the song of cliffs and clouds
summer rain that asks
where are your children
who clapped their hands like distant thunder
now the faint memories
echo in the secret stories they heard
the medicine of the feather and colored sand paintings
weaver and little sister
it is evening
old voice always sings
the low mummer remembering his name

ballad of the gutsy old lady i am becoming

it is just a song you know
perhaps you don't if you are young
just a song
aching after a lifetime with laughter lines
the kiss of gray
but such a voice . . .
words sung
out of a velvet longing
sultry wistful and lush

kentucky mystery

she must have been a hag of a woman
she and her moonshine still
i can almost see her—
bent and bending to tend the fire
talking to herself while the trees listened
        and whispered back
the broth would shimmer like her blood
                drop
                 by
                drop
                into a mason jar
            words come like that now
                burning the throat
                        of my inheritance

poetry helps, she said

for stacy, er nurse & poet

you scalpel your words into blood and
bone
until
breath appears between
the lines and spaces
then
each poem opens its white crane wings

and flies

muse

i am the voice who whispers . . .
when i speak   the words unfold
then dance in a single line
one after another as she listens . . .
i am the she of her
i am the mystery she cannot not follow
i am difficult as stone
i am easy as dust
i am indifferent to all she thinks she knows
yet mirror what she will learn to see
for i am her eyes   her breathing   her thirst
for i pound in her blood like moonshine

notes

"the final say"

My Jewish friend, Miriam, was in the hospital dying from a stroke. Her daughter and I were with her when she told the doctor to take out the IV and that she didn't want any efforts to help her continue to live. During one of the doctor's visits, we all had a discussion on how we wanted to die. The doctor was direct and to the point, "In my garden. Face down in the soil." Miriam died a week later. I had the honor to help bury her when I placed three shovels of warm earth on her casket.

"eight questions for eve after eden"

This poem was a 2020 Pushcart Prize nominee.

"writing the stars"

The poem tells of one of my childhood memories.

"for betty, with cancer, who asked for a poem"

Betty's hip cancer had been initially misdiagnosed. After she had received the news she had cancer, she came to visit us and stayed for supper. We serve buffet style in the convent dining room and I found myself standing behind her in line; she turned around and asked me, "Sister Lou, would you write a poem for me?" She died in 1999. Oddly enough, this poem would be the last one Betty, the poetry editor of *Byline Magazine*, would accept from me before she died of cancer.

"Shoah survivor defends immigrants in sacramento march 29, 2017"

Bernard Marks was a prisoner, beginning at age seven, in Auschwitz and Dachau. Of the two hundred of his family members who were also imprisoned, only five survived. Bernard confronted ICE director Thomas Homan and Sacramento Sheriff Scott Jones during a public forum concerning immigrants.

"encounter with anne sexton"

The university library was a fifteen-minute walk to the house where I was living with several other students. I remember it was a sunny afternoon and I was on my way home. I remember where I was standing when I heard the loud voices of children. A small dog, hit by a car, was reeling in agony. The children were watching at a safe distance. What I don't remember was how I found the pillow in a pile of cast-off material in the comer of a small upholstery shop close by. I also don't remember how I maneuvered the dog into the shop—pressing him down next to a door. Someone phoned for help and a man in blue truck arrived. The white sign on the door announced water department. My last memory of the event was watching the man carry the dog in the loop of his belt to his truck. I had discovered Anne Sexton's poetry that summer and during my reading I came across the nickname she had given herself: Mrs. Dog.

"when the sisters of mercy were nurses during the civil war"

Florence Nightingale trained several of the Sisters of Mercy who then went on to serve as nurses in the Civil War. Thanks to these sisters as well as those of other religious orders who also served, much of the wide anti-Catholic sentiment in the United States at that time greatly decreased.

On a personal note, I was born in a hospital the Sisters of Mercy staffed in 1949. Then, about a year or so after I entered the Catholic Church at sixteen, I met my first religious sister (nun) who was a Sister of Mercy. I decided to become a sister thanks to our friendship.

"on your blindness"

One of the local rabbis, Rabbi Sidney Wolf, was a great music lover who also taught music at Del Mar, Corpus Christi's junior college. He often sponsored concerts, one of which I attended at the synagogue where he was the rabbi. One my community sisters invited me to go with her to hear a blind singer who was studying music in New York City at that time. She shared her story with us before she began her program. She was a premature baby who needed oxygen treatments to help her live. However, the staff gave her too much which caused her blindness. The song I still remember her singing was Mozart's "Exsultate Jublilate."

"the retired lady at the texas assisted-living facility"

The image of the woman thanking me was an incident the night I entered the convent. My mother and I along with some of her friends had just stepped into the elevator when one of the oldest sisters in the community appeared and the elevator door remained opened long enough for her to tell me, "Thank you, thank you, a thousand times thank you." She was wearing coke-bottle bottom glasses and her cane would continue to glide her down the hallways until she died.

"judith slays holofernes"

This is the second poem I wrote on Judith—the first one was published in my book, *she: robed and wordless*. Tom Lombardo, my editor, continued to ask for a poem showcasing Judith's courage and determination to defend Bethulia, a town close to Jerusalem. The Assyrians, known for their cruelty, besieged the town for thirty-four days which resulted in a decision to surrender. Judith steps into the picture; upbraids those in power and declares she will take matters into her own hands. And she does so literally. Along with her maid, she kills the commander of the Assyrian army. Silk and beauty wielded a sword that saved a people.

"the unspeakable"

Even though I never met Sister Dianna Ortiz personally, I did "meet" her through an article someone had written about her years ago. However, I do remember the comment she made about forgiveness. I was very taken with her humility: that she could be so open about her struggle to live out the message of Jesus. Her death due to cancer was no surprise. Yet, her struggle to find meaning in her unspeakable experience inspired many people. She also struggled to shine a light on the 200,000 civilians who were also tortured and died in the 36-year civil war in Guatemala which in turn led her to become an advocate for torture victims throughout the world. The words I quoted as part of my poem were what I remembered and may not be totally accurate. I did find a similar quote in the online article, "Reclaiming My Soul After Torture." "Years have gone by since my torture, and I'm still unable to say if I have forgiven my torturers." She died on the Friday after Ash Wednesday in 2021. Rest in peace, dear saint, patron of those who struggle to forgive. The O.S.U. after her name means Order of St. Ursula which is the title/name of her religious community.

"giving voice to the thousands of missing and murdered indigenous women in the united states and canada"

As of 2014, the National Crime Information Center stated there were 5,712 reported cases of missing Indigenous women and girls in the United States. The Native Women's Association of Canada reported there are an estimated 4,000 missing women. This group did not give a date. However, the context suggests a similar date to the one in the United States.

.

"encounter with a Shoah survivor"

An ordinary trip to the post office would be my encounter with someone who survived the nightmare of the Shoah, or what most people refer to as the Holocaust.

I had visited the Holocaust Museum in Washington, D.C. as well as the one in Houston, Texas. I had researched World War II and the life of St. Edith Stein who was murdered in Auschwitz in 1942. I even visited the Yad Vashem in Jerusalem during my graduate theology study tour. However, this person in front of me was a survivor as my poem relates. For whatever reason when she put her left arm on the counter next to us, revealing its blue numbers tattooed in her flesh. The encounter was a gift and my poem, a humble attempt to say, "thank you." Thank you for sharing your life with me even if it was just for a moment.

"*unci maka*"

This is the Lakota name for grandmother earth. Lakota Elder, Virgil Taken Alive, approved of the poem, that is, it does not appropriate the culture of the First Peoples.

"*unci skan*"

This the Lakota name for grandfather sky. Virgil Taken Alive also approved of this poem.

"*poetry helps,* she said"

Several years ago, I chaired a panel for the People's Poetry Festival that was held on the Texas A & M Corpus Christi campus. I knew of Stacy Nigliazzo through Tom Lombardo, so I invited her to be on my panel where she could share her beautiful poetry. I took her to lunch afterwards. During our conversation, I asked, "How do you handle the pressures of being an ER nurse?" "Poetry helps," she said.

in gratitude

I would like to thank my religious community for giving me the time to write and for Sister Annette Wagner, OVISS, my former superior general, and Sister Anna Marie Espinosa. OVISS Regional Superior, who supported this project as well as Sister Maria de la Paz Padilla Rendón, OVISS, Superior General.

For Alice Berecka, who proofread my manuscript and for her friendship.

For Virgil Taken Alive, who took the time to read my First Peoples' poems and responded.

For Jeff Hermsen, who put me in touch with Virgil Taken Alive.

For those whose stories inspired me and are shared in this book.

For Tom Lombardo, my editor, and Kevin Watson, publisher.

And for the gift of faith that has sustained me.

Sister Lou Ella Hickman has a master's degree in theology from St. Mary's University in San Antonio, Texas, and is a former teacher and librarian. She is a certified spiritual director as well as a poet and writer. Her poems have appeared in numerous magazines including *America*, *First Things*, *Emmanuel*, *Third Wednesday*, and *new verse news*, and four anthologies: *The Night's Magician: Poems about the Moon*, edited by Philip Kolin and Sue Brannan Walker; *Down to the Dark River*, edited by Philip Kolin; *Secrets*, edited by Sue Brannan Walker; and *After Shocks: The Poetry of Recovery for Life-Shattering Events*, edited by Tom Lombardo. She has published many articles including seven in *Global Sisters Report* and was nominated for the Pushcart Prize in 2017 and 2020. Her first book of poetry, entitled *she: robed and wordless*, was published in 2015 by Press 53. Five poems from *she: robed and wordless* were set to music as *Chavah's Daughters Speak* by James Lee III and were performed on May 11, 2021, with opera soprano Susanna Phillips, principal clarinetist Anthony McGill of the New York Philharmonic, and two-time Grammy-nominated pianist Mayra Huang. The arrangement was part of a concert held at Y92 in New York City. At the time of this publication, other concerts were sponsored by the Cleveland Chamber Music Society, Washington Irving High School in New York City, the Dallas Chamber Music Society, the Philadelphia Chamber Music Society, Big Arts in Sanibel, Florida, and Clayton University in Morrow, Georgia.

About the Cover Artist

Cover artist Sister Marilyn Springs is a member of the Sisters of the Incarnate Word and Blessed Sacrament Order. Sister Marilyn was born in Buffalo, New York. She attended Our Lady of the Lake University in San Antonio, Texas where she received a Bacholar of Arts Degree. She later earned a Master's Degree in Catholic School Leadership from St. Mary's University also in San Antoino, Texas, as well as a PhD in Leadership Studies from St. Thomas University in Miami Gardens, Florida. Sister Marilyn has been painting for over thirty-five years and has taught art in elementary, middle school and high school levels. She specializes in portraits of women and children of color. The medium she prefers is acrylic due to its vibrant colors. Beginning in the school year, 2024, she will be principal at St. Joseph Elementary School in Yoakum, Texas.